The Goddess
and
The Gardener

Jane Whittle

The Goddess
and
The Gardener

Jane Whittle

Brigit's Forge

Published by Brigit's Forge
Gelli Fach, Clos y Ceiliog,
Llandre, SY24 5AN

Artwork by Jane Whittle ©

ISBN 978-0-9574106-1-9

Printed on FSC certified paper by Cambrian Printers Ltd.
www.cambrian-printers.co.uk

"Her garden... is so fragrant, verdant and peaceful, so enchanting in its look of settledness and in its caressing movements of shade and light, that entering it is to leave the troubles of the world behind. Visitors standing in the garden sometimes feel their hearts lock into place for an instant and experience blurred primal visions of creation - Eden itself, a paradise indeed. It is, you might say, her child, her dearest child, the most beautiful of her offspring, obedient but possessing the fullness of its spaces, its stubborn vegetable will. She may yearn to know the true state of the garden, but she wants even more to be part of its mysteries. She understands, perhaps, a quarter of its green secrets, no more. In turn it perceives nothing of her, not her history, her name, her longings, nothing - which is why she is able to love it as purely as she does, why she has opened her arms to it, taking it as it comes, every leaf, every stem, every root and sign."

From The Stone Diaries by Carol Shields. Quoted by permission of Carol Shields Literary Trust

To every gardener

and in memory of my father who first gave me a garden
and taught me how to plant seeds

To have been at one with the earth seems beyond undoing.
Rainer Maria Rilke

Contents

The Gardener

The Goddess

The Gardener

Return

I have returned to earth
completed many journeys.

Now it is time
to make a garden

in this untamed place,
to celebrate

and share
the growing ground

and find new strength
to stay at home.

Spring – Mozart in May

Here it is again
the growing season.
New arrivals
crowd their neighbours,
budding intermezzos
drown in brazen greens.

Already *now* is over
and the next day dusty.
Thin notes flicker
through the fragile poppies
as the primrose wilts.

Nothing repeats itself
like sound, a beat makes
petals drop, water trickles
through the music,
cools the sun-baked rocks.

Hot air rises with the tune,
invents a breeze
to swing un-practised leaves against the sky
and string green willow hair
through new-mown shade.

The oak trees glow
with gold and copper light
but green will flood them
when it rains
and bluebells fall.

The music never fails.
I can replay it
when the May moon changes,
celebrating birdsong, breezes,
green air, honeysuckle.

Wild notes die on violins
and bloom with woodwind,
driven on by
thunder and percussion,
cloudburst, rain beat – roses.

Summer – Writing in Bed

The summer wind moans in the passage,
rattling at windows and doors
a song of protection.

Safe in my bed I listen
as swallows click open the morning
after a night of rain.

I sleep late, after waking at cockcrow
to watch the sun rising.
But summer is hiding

in showers. Roses
and holiday makers
are taking their seasonal beating.

Water, in miniature rivers
of copper and silver,
falls from the feathers of fennel.

I look to your coming,
fill up the larder, clean the spare bedrooms,
plan projects and picnics

and save up my strength
for the mountains, for summer,
by lying in bed in the morning.

Autumn – Changing Skins

Accumulations of a summer's growth
drop off like habits
as all movement slows
and time expands into the shrinking light.

Colour has returned
to fill the silence of warm days
without a wind.
Birds begin new songs.

And I spread out again,
stretch like ripened fruit
until I burst
and let the old one go.

A week, or more,
and then I'm ready
to begin again.
Another summer's over.

Winter – And a Good Death.

Snow lies over my bones
resting in shadows.
Thin flakes land on my skin
and burn like departing stars.

This is an old month,
too tired to bear lambs.
The earth is hard on new flowers
broken by gales and frost.

I am dim as the view,
weak as a twig, pale as the sky.
I crack in the cold air
and return to the fire

remembering. Awake at night
at the low hour, unready to die,
I ask for more time
and less pain than you had,

an extension of quiet
in this kind land, days
with the young growing,
strength to complete my making

and a good death.

Sulis

Lady, I found you in wood,
whittled a piece of ash
pale enough for your skin,
leaving the rain-darkened bark
as your hair.

This is the place for you -
at the source of a faltering stream
where I listen for water,
intent on its flowing
close to young trees.

The moon floats in your mirror
under the willow,
its whispering leaves
finger our faces
while I wait for the Muse.

All the Bard's legendary trees
will grow in this garden -
hazel close by,
so those
nuts of wisdom
fall in the pool you are guarding.

Her Garden

It is an honour she allows -
to let me see her garden.
The magic must begin at home.

Outside grey air and winter greens
but, on the window, beads of rain
are fruit for leafless trees

and flowers for an empty field.
Her garden has preserved
the ground of dreams, un-weeded.

Here she stood and waited.
This is a place to share -
a place that two can manage.

Re-tracing outward paths,
returning home from other lands
I found her waiting

in the place we started from
among tall flowers.
The magic must begin at home.

There is

There is a tree
that waits for me
to stop
and search its branches
for the shapes I need.

There is a stone
I find to sit on
when I pause
and let my gaze rest
on the distant view.

There is a cat
that curls up
on my work
and purrs
until I listen.

There is a poem
I may write,
if I'm not thinking
and can hear it
singing.

The Lap

As an ageing gardener now
I let the seasons re-invent my days.
Rampaging out of April
energy returns like sap
to move more earth.

This Lap is not a throne,
but, set in secret
where a maze un-winds,
is made to seat a soul.

Where Rainbows Land

All colours spring
from where the rainbow lands.
When a rainbow took me in
its colours changed me.

Light split between us
as the rain cloud faced the sun,
uncovered brilliant rooms
with multi-coloured rafters.

A rainbow spanned
the gate that opened
and its double arch
contained my destination.

We knew we could not stand
beneath its halo,
but miracles come quietly now
I live where rainbows land.

Ty'r Ysgawen – The Place of Elders

These are the trees
that grow best
in this *place of elders,*
well-named and sheltered
from the north wind.

Fragile white blossom,
gathered in May-time,
is dainty as lace -
makes sparkling white wine
to tickle the tongue.

Blood-tasting berries,
picked on the last day
of the new moon
after the drought,
needed the rain.

Summer slipped by
without looking.
Robins were singing
too early,
apples reddened too soon.

Swallows were showing the young
which nests to return to,
getting lost in the river mist
which curled like a lamb's mother
turning to lick it.

Scalding and crushing
the wild fruits of autumn,
we add sugar and yeast
to their crimson juices.
They mature in the dark,

but return at the Solstice
to gladden our winter.
We pick them, destroy them
and brew them to brilliance.
Resurrected by firelight,

saved to be savoured,
they seep through our seasons;
bewitching out rhythms,
re-made and remembered,
they remind us of theirs.

She Is

She is a bell
ringing with new sounds.

She is a liquid
flowing in and out.

She is shining
through dark thickets.

She is flesh and bone
I can inhabit.

She has lent her many arms
to work with.

Sitting

Cut off, made firm
and left alone to root,
feel sap rising
at the annual flood.

Up through the stem
a surge from underground
to stretch the neck
and flicker at the finger ends -

a leaf uncurling,
opening like a flower
crowned with light, a wave of air
cascading in a cloak of rainbows.

Like a fountain, sitting here,
like a tree – well nurtured,
fed by sunlight, earth and air,
but not the source of water.

One Fine Morning

Children understand a garden.
They know each path
was made for following.

They talk to flowers,
make themselves at home in trees
and can't resist the water.

They communicate
with frogs and worms,
congregate on seats

and always seem to know
what was done with love -
or not.

Foxgloves

Foxgloves migrate in tribes,
march from place to place,
invade new territories each year
to occupy a chosen space
and preen together,
leaning out to peer at us
like football crowds.

Well-founded, patient, dressed alike,
these wide-mouthed watchers
set themselves in gardens
with a grace
too wild to cultivate.

The Goddess

In the Beginning

(*from an early Greek myth*)

The first darkness was solid,
thick with its own substance
but empty of music or motion.

> Then it stretched
> and I heard it.

I was there in the shudder and shriek
of its opening. Silence broke
into spaces that lightened my bones.

> So I rose
> out of chaos -

the Goddess of All Things
with so many names.
I came as Eurynome, naked

> and found there was nothing
> to stand on.

I divided the sea from the sky,
danced all alone on the waves
and made for the light in the south.

> Then a wind came
> and blew up behind me.

Was this something to play with -
a new and separate being
to help with the work of creation?

I whirled round
and caught it.

Holding it close I felt cold
so I rubbed it between my hands
and Behold! The North wind was a serpent!

I, Eurynome
inflamed him

by dancing ever more wildly
making warmth for my new body
and of the cold wind of chaos.

Ophion was moved
by my movement.

Roused, the great serpent Ophion
coiled himself seven times round me,
entwining us into one skin.

The Goddess, just so,
became pregnant.

I brooded over the waves
in the shape of a white dove
enduring the process of time

and then laid the Egg
of the Cosmos.

At my bidding Ophion, once more,
coiled himself seven times round it
and split the egg in two pieces.

> From this egg
> were hatched all my children.

Out of this egg, which I laid,
tumbled the countless children
born of the Goddess of All Things.

> Only a Goddess
> could do that -

bring forth the Sun and the moon and the stars
and the Earth with its mountains and oceans,
its trees and its herbs and its creatures.

> Quite soon,
> at home on Olympus,

I became vexed with Ophion,
for he claimed that He had created
the Cosmos – un-aided,

> So I stamped
> on his head,

I kicked out his teeth
and banished him into the darkness
for ever.

> Then I created
> planetary powers,

setting a pair of giants
over the Sun and the Moon and five planets
and giving them names.

> But those names
> were soon changed.

The first people sprung
from the soil where the serpent's teeth
landed, and seeded.

> A dragon rose there
> to guard them.

They built huts, they made garments,
learned to find food and use fire.
Those were our first children.

Her Return

I returned with water,
skimming over waves
that stream in from the West,
embraced by sunsets.

I rode the flickered moon face
in the shadow pool
where the weeping willow
winds leaves through my hair.

Wind and water
thunder with my singing,
rain and dew-fall
bring my blessing.

Now cities, forests, dreams
lie waste – re-plant
and tend
a garden.

I Lay Down

I lay down
and became land
where long waves breasted
a green shore.

I was there
when ancient trees
were buried under shifting sands
and drenched by surging tides.

Rocks were smoothed
by water and wind
and stones were cleared
from the land.

I watched over
the mapping of moons,
the march of the sun
and the counting of stars.

Then I slept
through various visions,
lay hidden
for thousands of years.

I awake to remind you
of forgotten paths
and how to unblock
ancient springs.

Feel my breath
on a warm wind,
meet my eye
in the moon.

Lay yourself down
and become land.
Listen -
you will hear me.

I Am

I am the tree
that waits for you
to search my branches
for the shapes you need.

I am the rock
you sit on when you rest
and let your gaze
merge with the view.

I am the cat
that curls up on your work
and purrs
until you listen.

I am the poem
you will write
when you're not thinking
and can hear it singing.

Dawn

As glory gilds my sides
green shades my burning.

The gold of day invades
the muffled indigos

where seeds are curling.
I rest upon the shore -

a hill surprised by morning.
My hair flows on the tide

and, scattered on the sand,
wet rocks are set like jewels

in those shadow shapes
the rising sun reverses.

You wake to see a world re-born,
embodied differently by dawn.

Gaia

I am old.
One side aches as I turn,
I'm too heavy to rise
and unbend my bones.

Rock was my bed for too long,
but the soil under my limbs
will grow grass,
limp in the heat, flattened by rain;

and the wild gold can root high,
dance on a warm wind
and flow like an ocean
meeting the sky.

I am stroked
by the bruising clouds,
washed and brushed while I sleep
undisturbed by their storms.

I wait for the birds
to return in good time,
formations come home bearing fish,
or a flurry of flocks

swing on an empty field -
a dish of liquid tipped into light,
suddenly flooded again
by relentless dawn.

The spiral I follow is air,
currents repeating themselves.
I am burned up or frozen,
re-spun like a star

flowing through space,
a river re-forming its banks,
shifting oceans and shores,
re-building the hills.

But every seed sown
and every root grown
to make leaves
must be offered to rain.

As I turn and re-turn,
I return you to life
under the same sky.
Remember my story.

Her Song

I am a fish with a golden tail,
I flicker so fast you miss me.

I am a tree with silver leaves
turned by invisible winds.

I am the brilliance of a wave
so bright it makes you blink.

I am the rock too heavy to move
until you give up trying.

I am a flower, a petal, a seed
in soil, in rain, in sunlight,

in your blood, your bones and your breath -
listen to my message!

I am there when you are alone,
we are alone together.

Watch the space between the clouds,
the pause in breath, or footsteps.

In the Silence

In the silence, after singing,
you have felt your ear bones ringing.

You have seen me flying high
in an empty summer sky -

green eyes under clouds of hair
a naked lady made of air.

Full moon with the sun still burning -
the Equinox – the whole earth turning

as you stand on it below.
Remember what you used to know.

Dream Walker

Once a green goddess
went walking on these hills.

Her garments hugged her
like a flowing river

and the Southwest wind
blew in from the sea

to warm itself
against her contours.

Above the Bay
she reached an open place
as green as she was
and lay down there

to let the land absorb her bones
while she diluted sunlight,

left her shadow, like a wind-bent tree,
to fit the sloping hillside.

You see it flowing over walls,
un-lacing boundaries.

She left her shape here
lying on the warm earth

wrapped in gorse and heather,
while her hair – a halo –
grew and spread
into a web of light

which stretches everywhere
you feel her presence.

I

I am the rock rain batters at;
water runs along my runnels,
settles in my hollows
and smooths the sharpest edge.

I am the tree the wind conducts,
up-turning leaves and tearing twigs,
made to dance
the wildest jigs.

I am the flower dawn discovers
opening to light and dew.
As petals fall
they prophesy the fruit.

I am the cave beneath the rock,
the space between the branches
and inside the seed.
I contain and am contained

            by emptiness.